SIZE, DISTANCE, WEIGHT

THE DRAWING OF THE SUN WHICH APPEARS ON THE JACKET AND THE DRAWING AT THE
TOP OF PAGE 28 ARE REPRODUCED BY PERMISSION OF THE BETTMANN ARCHIVE, INC.

SIZE, DISTANCE, WEIGHT

A First Look at Measuring

BY SOLVEIG PAULSON RUSSELL

ILLUSTRATED BY

MARGOT TOMES

HENRY Z. WALCK, INCORPORATED   NEW YORK

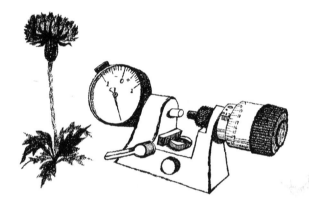

WHAT DOES MEASURING MEAN?

Everything we can see has size and weight. Some things are big and heavy, some are so small and light we cannot feel any weight to them. But even a single hair or a piece of dandelion fuzz can be weighed. They can be measured to show how wide and how long each is, too.

Whenever we answer questions such as "How big is it?" "How long is it?" "How heavy is it?" "How fast does it go?" we are using measurement.

Because we need the answers to such questions
in our lives—when we build things, or cook, when
we plan trips, or go shopping, in a million every-
day things—measuring is very important.

MEASURING DISTANCE

Distance is the space from one thing to another —the space from the ceiling to the floor, from Maine to Florida, or even from one end of a pencil to the other. From your feet to the top of your head is distance, and when you walk from one end of a room to the other, the space you cover is distance, too.

We measure distances to see how far apart things are—how much distance is between them. We want to know how tall a person is, how far it is from home to school or to the moon, how wide a table is, how high a ladder will reach.

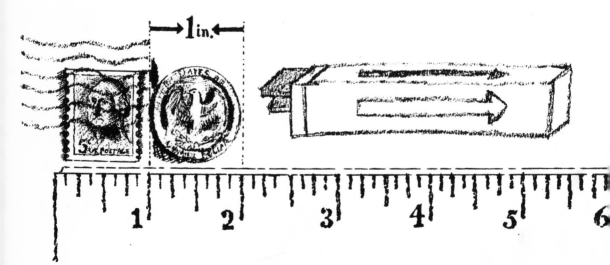

One tool for measuring distance is the ruler. If you look at a ruler, you will see that it is marked off into parts by straight lines. Each part is the distance of one inch (the shorter lines mark off fractions or smaller parts of inches). An inch is about the width of an ordinary postage stamp. A quarter is about an inch across. A stick of gum is three inches long. A dollar bill is about six inches long.

The most common ruler is 12 inches long. It is called a foot ruler, for 12 inches equals one foot. A foot is as long as four sticks of gum laid end to end. It is as long as a large phonograph record is across. It is as far as the distance straight through a football, from one tip to the other.

Most adults are between five and six feet tall. There are 90 feet between the bases on a baseball diamond.

12 inches = 1 foot

If you put three foot rulers in a line, you would see the distance called a yard. A yard is three feet, or 36 inches long. A ruler that is a yard long is sometimes called a yardstick. A yard is about as high as most kitchen stoves or sinks. A football field is one hundred yards long, from one goal line to the other, and fifty yards wide.

$$3 \text{ feet} = 1 \text{ yard}$$

A rod is a measure of distance that is not often used by most people. A rod is the same distance as 16½ feet. It is used in measuring land.

Imagine how long a line of 5,280 foot rulers would be if they were placed end to end. They would stretch for about 20 blocks of some cities.

They would stretch a mile. A mile is the name of
the distance that is 5,280 feet long. Miles are measures for long distances.

$$16\tfrac{1}{2} \text{ feet} = 1 \text{ rod}$$
$$5{,}280 \text{ feet} = 1 \text{ mile}$$

Farm land is usually measured by acres. An acre
is an area of land a little smaller than a football field.

MEASURING WEIGHT

Measuring distance is only one of the ways we can measure. Some people are tall, but thin. Others, just as tall, may be quite a bit fatter. These people aren't the same size, except in their height. They weigh different amounts.

A box of corn flakes and a box of nails may be the same size, but the box of nails will be much heavier than the box of corn flakes. A bag of grain is heavier than a bag of feathers. When two children play on a see-saw, one end of the see-saw will go down if one child is much heavier than the other. Sometimes two smaller children on one end will balance a larger, heavier child.

To see how heavy something is, we weigh it—we measure its weight. Scales are the tools used for measuring weight. In fruit and vegetable stores there are often scales for weighing. The scales are usually hanging pans with a dial of numbers at the top. When something is put in the pan the pan moves downward because of the weight in it. This pulls a part of the scales that moves the pointer on the dial. The pointer stops at a number on the dial to show the amount of weight in the pan.

Platform scales are also used in stores. When goods are placed on the platform, or shelf, a pointer shows the weight on a dial.

It takes large scales to measure heavy things like trucks. The trucks are driven onto weighing platforms set into the ground and are then weighed.

Some people have scales at home to weigh themselves. These have platforms to stand on, with a pointer to show the weight.

Scientists have scales that can weigh things so small we cannot see them easily. They can tell how much just one inch of a piece of hair from your head weighs. They can measure the weight of things much smaller than a piece of hair.

We most often weigh things by ounces, pounds, and tons.

An ounce is a small weight measure. A package of candy lifesavers weighs about an ounce. A medium-sized egg weighs about two ounces.

Sixteen ounces is the same amount of weight as one pound. If you think of how heavy a pound of butter or margarine is you will have a good idea of a pound weight. A newborn baby weighs about seven pounds.

Sometimes people use the word "hundredweight" when they are talking about 100 pounds.

A ton is a measure used for very heavy measuring. It stands for 2,000 pounds.

People who buy coal sometimes buy it in ton measurements. Grain, and potatoes, and other crops farmers raise, are often sold by the ton too.

A fully grown elephant may weigh four tons. Ocean liners and the dirt dug from the earth to make basements weigh many times 2,000 pounds —many tons.

16 ounces = 1 pound

2,000 pounds = 1 ton

J. Mc. ILLHENNY & SONS
COAL & GRAIN

MEASURING VOLUME, or CAPACITY

The volume, or capacity, of anything means how much it holds. Boxes, pots and pans, cans, tanks, bottles, swimming pools, trucks, and a great many other containers all have volume, or space that something can go into. Everyone who builds or makes a container of any kind must know how much it will hold. Those who buy filled containers want to know how much they are buying, too.

At home, your mother measures with cups, tablespoons, and teaspoons. These are measures of volume used in cooking. But for usual measuring we have two sets of common volume measures. One set is for measuring dry things. One set is for measuring liquids. Both these sets use two of the same measures—pints and quarts.

Dry measures are pints, quarts, pecks, and bushels.

You will have a good idea of how much a pint is if you think of how much two measuring cups would hold, because that amount is a pint. Two pints, or four cupfuls, make a quart.

There are eight quarts in a peck, and four pecks in a bushel. A bushel will hold the same amount as a big box of apples.

These dry measures are used to measure fruits, some vegetables such as potatoes, and grains. In some areas of the country the measures are heaped on top. In other places they are filled just level with the top edge.

2 pints = 1 quart
8 quarts = 1 peck
4 pecks = 1 bushel

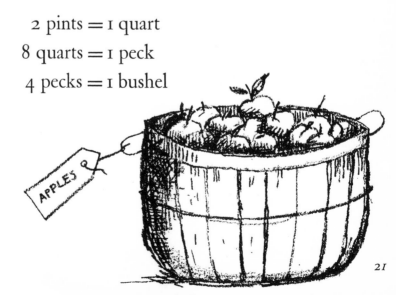

Liquid measures are pints, quarts, and gallons. There are two pints in a quart, and four quarts, or eight pints, in a gallon.

We buy milk by liquid measures. When you help bring the milk into your home notice the size of the bottles or containers. When you drink two glasses of milk from glasses that hold as much as a measuring cup you have had a pint of milk. Four such glasses would hold a quart.

One of the products that many people buy by the gallon is gasoline for their cars. When we buy gasoline the pump at the service station measures the gasoline into the car. The pump shows the number of gallons of gasoline that go through the filling hose.

2 pints = 1 quart

4 quarts = 1 gallon

MEASURING TIME

If we had no way to measure time we would never know just when to get to school, or meet a friend, or how long to cook an egg. Work time, school time, train time, would be any time. There would be no order in our lives.

There is order because we know how to measure time. We have clocks and calendars to help us. A clock is a tool, or a machine, with a face that is divided up into parts by lines and, usually, by the numbers from one to twelve. On the clock face there are two hands, a short—or hour—hand and a long —or minute—hand. There are millions of clocks of all sizes; large ones on buildings, wall clocks, desk

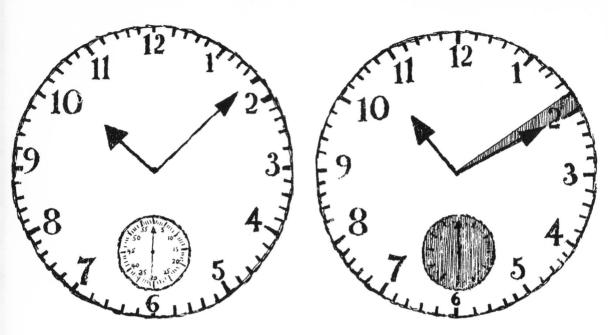

clocks, and small watches. But they all measure time in the same way.

On many clocks there is another hand, called the second hand, that goes racing around the clock face or around a small dial on the face. If you watch the second hand move you see that it doesn't take long for it to make a complete trip around the clock's face. It takes just one minute. A second is about as long as it takes you to say "second." There are 60 seconds in a minute.

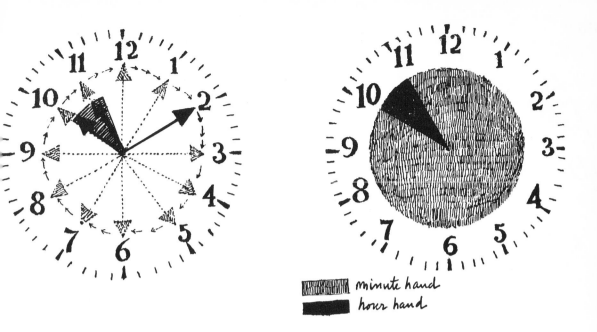

minute hand
hour hand

While the second hand ticks 60 times on its round trip, the long minute hand moves only a very small distance. It moves one minute. When the minute hand has moved through 60 minutes it has gone around the clock face once.

In the time it takes the minute hand to go around, the small hour hand has moved only between two numbers on the clock face. So we see that it takes 60 minutes to make one hour, just as it takes 60 seconds to make one minute.

There are 24 hours in a whole day, including nighttime and daytime. There are 12 hours between midnight and noon and 12 hours between noon and midnight.

$$60 \text{ seconds} = 1 \text{ minute}$$
$$60 \text{ minutes} = 1 \text{ hour} \text{ ,}$$
$$24 \text{ hours} = 1 \text{ day}$$

A calendar is another tool for telling time, but it does not tell about the length of a day. A calendar is a chart or way of keeping track of the days and months that make up a year.

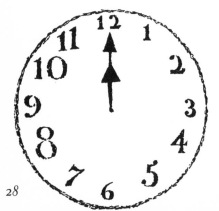

There are seven days in one week—Sunday, Monday, Tuesday, Wednesday, Thursday, Friday, and Saturday. Fifty-two weeks make up a year.

There are 12 months in a year—January, February, March, April, May, June, July, August, September, October, November, and December. Most of the months have 31 days, but September, April, June, and November have only 30 days. February has 28 days, except in leap years when February has 29 days. There are 365 days in a year, and 366 days in a leap year.

$$24 \text{ hours} = 1 \text{ day}$$
$$7 \text{ days} = 1 \text{ week}$$
$$12 \text{ months} = 1 \text{ year}$$

JANUARY

S	M	T	W	T	F	S
	1	2	3	4	5	6
7	8	9	10	11	12	13
14	15	16	17	18	19	20
21	22	23	24	25	26	27
28	29	30	31			

MEASURING HEAT

In summertime we are often very warm. In the winter we need warm clothes to keep comfortable. We need heat in our homes for wintertime comfort, too. Whether we feel warm or cold depends on the temperature, which is the amount of heat there is to be measured. Besides needing heat for comfort, people use heat in other ways. Cooking is one of these ways. Making things in factories, and working out science problems are other uses of heat.

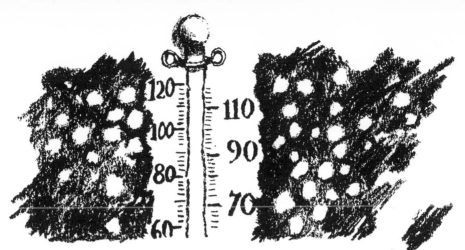

A thermometer is the tool we use for telling how hot or cold anything is. Thermometers are glass tubes with a little of a substance called mercury in them. When it is warm mercury swells and rises in the tube. When it is cold the mercury shrinks and goes down the tube.

There are numbers on, or beside, every thermometer tube. The numbers mark small distances called degrees on the thermometer. By reading the numbers at the level of the mercury, you can tell the temperature in degrees.

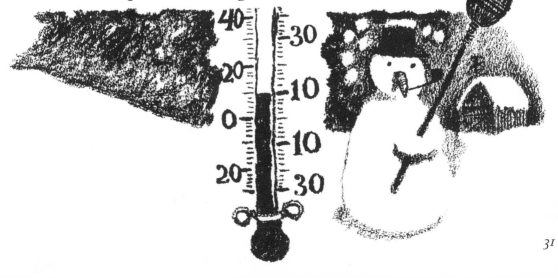

There are two kinds of thermometers. The one we see most often is called the Fahrenheit thermometer. On this thermometer, water will boil when the mercury rises to 212 degrees. Water would freeze when the mercury measures 32 degrees. The thermometer used to take a person's temperature is a Fahrenheit thermometer. Normal body temperature is 98.6 degrees. Room thermometers, or outdoor thermometers, are usually Fahrenheit too.

Scientists use a second kind of thermometer, called the centigrade thermometer. It works just like the Fahrenheit one, but the scale of numbers is different. On a centigrade thermometer water boils at 100 degrees and freezes at 0 degrees.

In order to tell which thermometer is being used, the letter F. or C. is written after the number of degrees. F. stands for Fahrenheit. C. stands for

centigrade. Instead of writing the word "degree," a small circle may be drawn near the upper right part of the number.

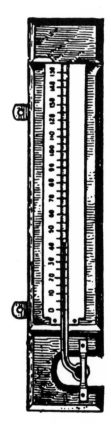

METERS

In front of the driver in every car there is a glass-covered dial called a speedometer. It has a hand, or marker, that moves to tell how fast the automobile is going. When the car speeds up the speedometer pointer moves to a higher number.

The last part of the word "speedometer" is meter. Every meter is a measuring tool, used for measuring something.

Parking meters measure the time a car is parked when money is put into them to start them working.

Electricity meters measure the amount of electricity used in a building.

The water that flows from outside pipes into a home is measured by a water meter.

If your family uses a gas stove, or gas heat, the gas is measured by a gas meter.

It is interesting to see how far you walk in an hour, or a day. There are meters called pedometers that can measure the distance. Pedometers can be carried in a pocket, or worn on a belt. As a person walks the movement of his body makes the meter work.

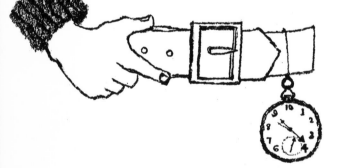

OTHER MEASURES

In this book we have talked about measures that almost all people use, or need. But there are many other types of measures. Scientists, sailors, jewelers, and many other people use special measures in their work.

Scientists have tools or machines to measure light, the force of winds and heartbeats, the growth of parts of plants and animals, and countless other things.

Sailors and seamen use measures to tell where they are in the ocean, and all the many ways the different parts of their ship engines are working. Two measurements that we sometimes hear about are fathoms and knots. A fathom is the same as six feet in distance. Fathoms are used to measure the depth of water. A knot is a measure of the speed a ship is traveling.

6 Feet

12 Feet

18 Feet

Jewelers who work with diamonds and other precious stones use a measurement called a carat. It takes about 152 carats to equal one ounce of weight. Sometimes the carat is spelled with a K instead of a C.

A carat in gold measuring is not a measure of weight. It is a measure of parts. It shows how many parts of gold there are in a mixture of metals. If you see gold jewelry that is marked 10 carat (or 10K) you will know that there are 10 parts of pure gold in it and 14 parts of other metal. The number of parts of gold and other metals together must equal 24 parts.

THE METRIC SYSTEM

Most of the countries of the world do not use the same measures as we use. They do not use inches, feet, miles, pints, quarts, gallons, pounds, tons, bushels, or other such measurements. They have a simpler way of measuring things. It is called the metric system.

The metric system has three main measurements. They are:

the gram for measuring weight

the meter for measuring distance

the liter for measuring capacity

A gram weighs very little—just a bit more than one-thirtieth of an ounce. A dime weighs a little more than two grams and a nickel weighs five grams. A half dollar weighs eleven and a half grams.

A meter is a little more than 39 inches long. If you think of a distance three inches longer than a yardstick you will know about how long it is.

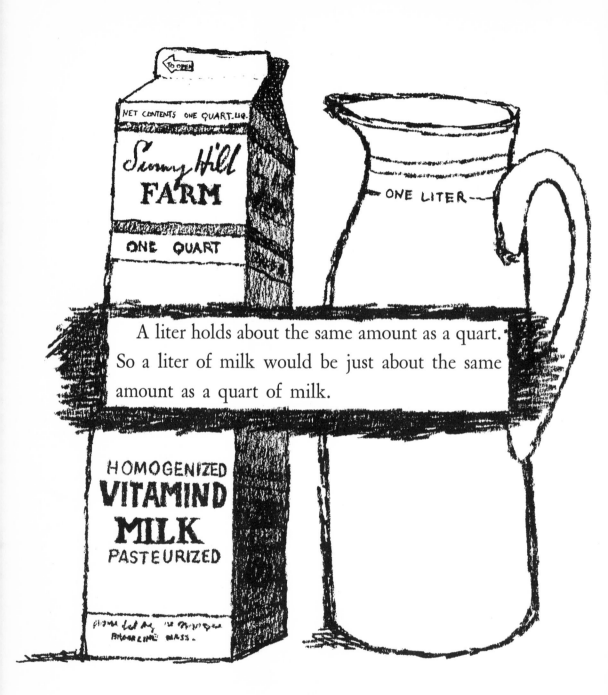

NET CONTENTS ONE QUART LIQ.

Stony Hill
FARM

ONE QUART

ONE LITER

A liter holds about the same amount as a quart. So a liter of milk would be just about the same amount as a quart of milk.

HOMOGENIZED
VITAMIND
MILK
PASTEURIZED

All measurements of greater amounts of any of these measures are figured by increasing each one by ten, or a hundred, or a thousand times itself. There are three beginnings of words to show these increases. The three word beginnings are:

deca, which means 10

hecto, which means 100

kilo, which means 1000

Decagram means ten grams; hectogram means a hundred grams; kilogram means a thousand grams.

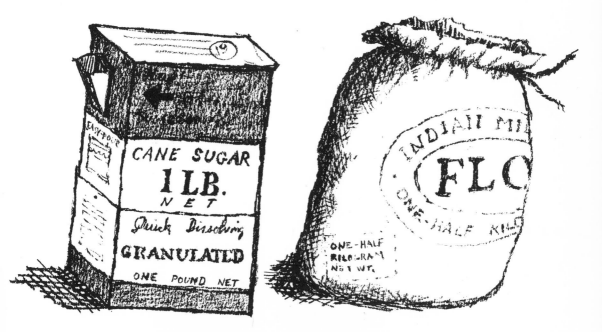

All measuring amounts smaller than whole grams, meters, or liters are shown by three beginnings of words, too. These show that the measure is divided by ten, a hundred, or a thousand. These word beginnings are:

deci, which means 1/10

centi, which means 1/100

milli, which means 1/1000

Decigram means a tenth part of a gram; centigram means a hundredth part of a gram; milligram means a thousandth part of a gram.

To use the metric system, you need to know only the gram, the meter, and the liter, and the six word beginnings. With these measures any weight, distance, or volume can be shown.

Many manufacturers in our country put metric measurements on the labels of things they sell. If you look at the packages of such things as raisins, baking powder, and spices, you will probably see these metric measurements on the labels. Metric measurements are frequently given on cereal, and on vitamin packages, and on drugs.

For years many people have thought that our country should change to the metric system of measuring because it is easier to use, and most of the rest of the world uses it. It is used now by scientists in our country as well as by all scientists in other parts of the world. Perhaps some day the metric system will be used for all measuring in this country, too.

In earliest times, men used parts of their bodies
for measures. A foot, a thumbnail, an armlength,
or a pace were used to measure distance. Men
weighed things by holding a different object in
each hand and guessing which was heavier. Later,
two objects were hung from the ends of a stick; the
heavier object would pull its end down. Over the
centuries, our systems of measurement were developed.

Today, men are learning to measure in wonderful new ways. With new measuring tools scientists can measure the length of time since dinosaurs roamed our world. They can measure the distance to stars, and make satellites in space obey commands from stations on earth. They can measure things smaller than a millionth of an inch, and send television pictures from one part of the world to another far distant part in minutes. Computers —wonderful measuring machines—can give answers to number problems in a few moments that would take a person many years to figure.

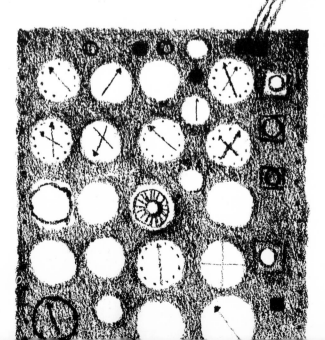

Yet these measuring techniques, remarkable as they are, are just the beginnings of many others still to be developed.

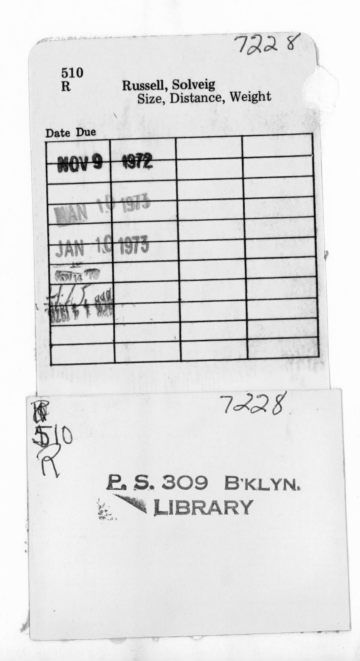